I am your friend

a book of hope

Billie Bacall

Here it is!

The much requested pocketbook
edition of 'I AM YOUR FRIEND'.

Purposefully designed to fit in the
palm of your hand and be the
perfect companion when you
are out and about.

The complete collection can be
found in the hardback edition
of 'I AM YOUR FRIEND'.

FUTUREDREAMS

FOR THOSE TOUCHED BY BREAST CANCER

20% of the profits of this publication will
be donated to the charity Future Dreams
www.futuredreams.org.uk

First Published © 2018 by Doverlake, London
www.iamyourfriendbook.co.uk

ISBN 978-1-99931-790-4

A catalogue record for this book is
available from the British Library.

The right of Billie Bacall to be identified as the author
of this work has been asserted by him in accordance with
the Copyright, Designs and Patents Act, 1988.

Book design by adamhaystudio.com

FOR
E, M, Y & J

THANK YOU
Agnies Calkoen, Dr Gowri Motha & Carole Murray
for your invaluable guidance
&
Kate Rowe-Jones

preface

I know how it feels to be down, locked in an internal world of painful thoughts. Within the space of a couple of years, I experienced the sudden death of my husband, major surgery and embarked on a course of chemotherapy.

What can help the human spirit in moments like this? Sometimes just a spark, a detail, a word, an image can lift the mood. In the space of a breath it is possible to change the way you feel.

I did not plan to create this collection; rather it emerged through this period of my life. Feeling isolated and fearful I started to jot down fleeting images to cheer myself up. Recollections: an inspiring thought here, a word there, a feeling would ignite an expression from myself.

So, Dear Friend.
The purpose of this book is to help elevate your spirits in such moments. Even if only one small detail makes you smile and inspires you, then its purpose has been achieved.

London
November 2018

Never give up

No matter what is going on

Never give up
Develop the heart
Be Compassionate
Not just to your friends
But to everyone
Be Compassionate

Work for Peace
In your heart
And in the World
Work for Peace
And I say again
Never give up

No matter what is going on

Never
give
up

Words attributed to His Holiness the 14th Dalai Lama

I'm just having a blip...

Blow Away The
Pain + Sadness

Gone

there

is

always

light

at

the

end

of

the

tunnel

HOPE
is the
better
option . . . . .

hope

despair

images

IT ALL

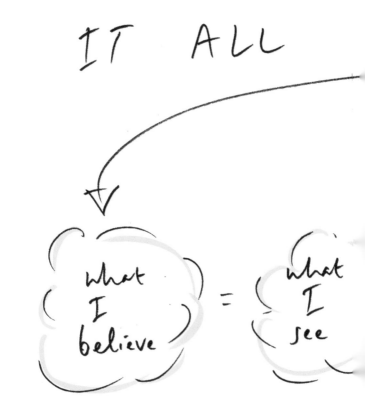

what
I
believe = what
I
see

STARTS HERE

= what I experience

Fall in Love with the Process.

LIFE THIS WAY ⟶

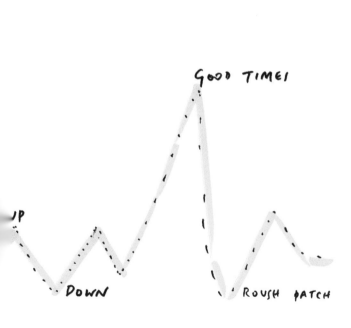

U Have Everything
Here To Be Happy ！

life is an
adventure......

love

how exciting!

my future is open...

done that!

new things!

which way?

direct
your inner compass

To a Beautiful
Destination !

amazing
things
are coming
my way!

I'm
Done
With
All
That...

R ise UP

its Cool to be Kind!

APPRECIATE
the

small pleasures

stay
in
THiS
moment

next

next

Think
ouT
the
Box

Think
Possibilities!

possibilities

<u>not</u>

~~Limitations~~

Stay connected
to those
U Love !!!

..... gaze into
the darkness...

and feel
PE ACE
not
fear

stay on the sunny

side of the street..

Don't be influenced by others.....!!!!!

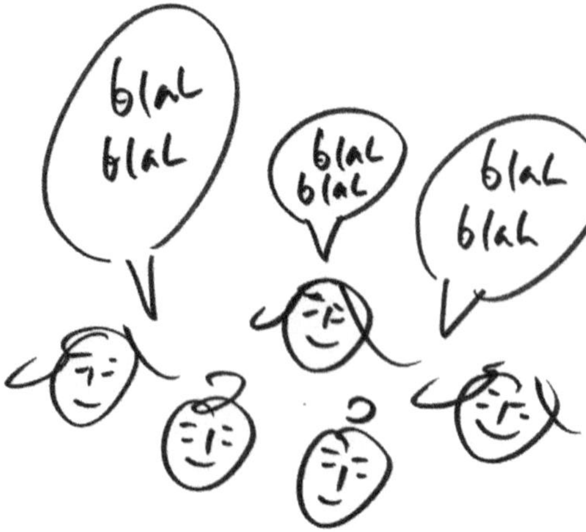

DUDE!

U

R

Beautiful!!!

Let your spirit shine

and
become
the
light
for all
those
around
you

epilogue

Your beliefs become your thoughts

Your thoughts become your words

Your words become your actions

Your actions become your habits

Your habits become your values

Your values become your destiny

Words attributed to Mahatma Ghandi

inner

Find Your Way...

peace

To Create Your Own..

FUTUREDREAMS

FOR THOSE TOUCHED BY BREAST CANCER

Future Dreams was established in 2008 by mother and daughter Sylvie Henry and Danielle Leslie, when by a cruel twist of fate they were both diagnosed with breast cancer. Tragically, both women lost their lives to the disease within a year of each other in 2009. Their dream was to make sure that nobody should ever have to face this illness on their own.

Future Dreams pledges funds towards the charity's three divisions: support, awareness and research, focusing on secondary breast cancer. Working closely with Breast Cancer Haven to fund vital support centres; with Breast Cancer Care to promote awareness; and with Breast Cancer Now to fund specific research projects toward the goal that by 2050, everyone diagnosed will live.

20% of the profits of this publication will be donated to Future Dreams – www.futuredreams.org.uk